Grace and Truth

Grace and Truth

The Twin Towers of the Father's Heart

Stan DeKoven, Ph.D.

Copyright ©2012 Stan E. DeKoven

ISBN 978-1-61529-033-8

Contents

Contents	i
Forward	v
Author's Forward	ix
Introduction	xiii

1 The Grace that Dwells with Us — 1
  The Grace that Dwells 3
  Important Consideration 7

2 Moses: The Plan of Salvation — 9
  The Significance of the Tabernacle: A Place of Presence or Authority Heaven on Earth . . 12
  The Tabernacle: Presentation of God's Redemptive Plan 15

3 David's Tent — 19
  A Pattern of Worship for Future Generations . 19
  The Tabernacle of David: A Present Application 20
  What is Davidic Worship? 21
  Key Chapters Regarding the Tabernacle of David 22
  A Sign of the Last Days 23

4	The Temple of Solomon	25
	Jesus: The Tabernacle of Grace and Truth	
	Some Examples of Grace Personified . . .	28
	Grace Indeed	29
	An Important Parable of Two	30
	An Application	31

5	The Grace that Manifests the Father's Glory	35
	What does it mean to manifest the glory? . . .	35
	Revealing the Father - Old Testament	36
	The Father Revealed from Old to New Testament	38
	New Testament Revelation of the Father	39
	Learning to Share	39

6	The Grace Upon Grace for Us	43
	What Price Must You Pay for His Grace? . . .	43
	His Grace, Our Graciousness	46

7	The Grace of Truth for Us: Truth or Consequences	49
	Get in the Flow	54

8	Results of Grace and Truth: Freedom and Transformation	57
	Being Who You Already Are	59

9	Grace and Truth: We Can't Live Without Them	63
	More on Grace	64
	What is Truth?	66

10	Conclusion	69
	Grace and Truth: The Twin Towers of the Father's Heart	69
	A Final Look	70

Epilogue 71

About the Author **77**

Forward

One of the things I have noticed in Western Christianity has been a lack of depth and maturity in its teaching, and in many ways this is the blight on the people of God. To me, one of the keys to the Kingdom is capturing who we already are in Christ, which has been established and sealed forever in heaven by the finished work of Calvary. Jesus has forever secured the people called by His name as "The Royal Priesthood". Coming to terms with this is not only the believer's right, but also the way to living in victory.

After being saved, through a wonderful work of grace in my heart, and having full assurance of faith through that same grace, I felt that I needed to do something and earn my salvation. How ridiculous! This led me to "professional" Christianity, where I did things because I knew they were the right things to do. Further, my behaviors seemed to get the right responses from my peers and the people of faith. In so many ways this led me to a faithless Christian walk, rather than into whom Christ had sealed me to be. It seems that this is the way for believers.

But being a person with an inquisitive heart with a stubborn Irish background, it caused me to reassess who I am in Him. I realize that He has cancelled the written code of the law that separated me from Him, and has made me alive in Him, in spite of errors in my walk.

Forward

When we, as children of the living God, get a hold of the fact that nothing can, has, or will separate us from God, we can really start to live by faith and take risks because we realize God will not punish us for trying.

I remember when my son and daughter were first learning to walk. They would stagger a few steps and then stumble, grasping for anything that was close, as they ungraciously fell to the floor, dragging with them whatever their little hands could take. Do you think for a moment that I leapt to my feet and chastised them for trying and making a mess of it. No. I would simply smile and encourage their next adventure. To think that our heavenly Father, who not only gives love but IS love, would do anything different is preposterous. I now know that He is beside me in all that I do, encouraging those leaps of faith that I undertake.

In Galatians 3:29 it says:

> "And if you are Christ's, then you are Abraham's seed and heirs according to the promise."

The least of these words in the previous scripture are two of the most important words, IF and THEN. If we are Christ's then we are Abraham's seed, and we inherit everything that He inherits from the Father. Incredibly, the most important relationship for the people of faith is not them and their spouse or church or even with God. It is the relationship between Jesus and His Father, because we inherit everything in that relationship. To understand and comprehend the fullness of this relationship may require significant relearning and adjustments of the beliefs we have held dear. We may even have to move beyond what we have felt secure with in the past. To know this truth by experience, leads us to realize that faith is never passive but active. It takes us into a new realm of living that overtakes all the other facets of life.

From a review of the life of Abraham, we can see that it was in an act of obedient faith, whereby he left what he knew and entered into the unknown where God met him and he was changed. Our belief and belonging are no different. It is in going and obedience that God meets us at every turn. Our salvation and rest is not based upon rights and wrongs but upon belief and belonging. Living in the realm of the supernatural is based on an understanding of what Christ has done for us - in other words, becoming what we already are! You may feel like you are in many ways, like Gideon or David, "The least of your tribe," but it makes a difference to the world when we know who we are and who stands with us as we walk the walk of faith.

It is with great delight that I write this for my dear friend and brother, Dr Stan DeKoven. He has captured succinctly and fluently the Grace and Truth of God's Kingdom in such a way that if the reader takes a hold of it by faith, they can take a step closer to being who they already are!

> Pastor Rob Cunningham, M.A.
> Senior Pastor
> The Promise Centre
> Wagga Wagga NSW Australia.

Author's Forward

With the words of the song "God Bless the USA" by Lee Greenwood still resounding in my ears, I am reminded that yearly the American people remember the events of September 11, 2001. We commemorate all that was lost on the anniversary of that dreadful day. It was the day when the Twin Towers, representing American material strength, power, and prestige; came crashing down. To many, the towers were symbolic of our identity as US citizens. It also represented who we were as a nation in terms of the global community and the influence we enjoyed with other world powers.

In our country, a great deal of faith has been placed in the power of our wealth and military might, both in the past and in the present. At one time this power was  deemed as invincible. We now know better. As believers, we know intuitively not to put our trust in mammon which is the biblical term for the world system.

It would be insightful to revisit the events of history that led this country into its position of power and prosperity. To better understand the significance of the tow-

Author's Forward

ers, we need to rediscover the roots from which the citizens of the United States have come.

The original settlers arrived on the eastern coast of this beautiful country to establish a colony at Plymouth Rock in pursuit of their religious freedom. They wanted the freedom to worship the Lord as they wished, without governmental interference. We know that freedom was not easily won, for many lost their lives in the process of establishing their colony. Nevertheless the battle was fought and the victory obtained through sheer persistence, dedication, and devotion to the Lord.

The dedication of these founding fathers to the Lord was evidenced by the words we find etched upon our currency. It states, "In God We Trust." Because the very establishment of this country was based upon the right to serve the Lord, God blessed it. The proof of God's blessing is evident by the power, prestige, and influence this country has experienced. The Twin Towers are representative of the success of this great nation in the pursuit of its happiness, but perhaps even more importantly, the right to serve the Lord in freedom. God blesses those who put Him first.

The towers may have been important symbols representing the success of the United States, but the attackers robbed us of the symbols, not our true identities. No one can take away our identity. They cannot erase the knowledge of who we are. In the words of our founding fathers we are, "One nation under God." Any who have an identity rooted in God, need not fear. Our identity as God's children is safe and sound in his loving arms.

As much as I love the United States and still grieve over the loss of the 9/11 victims, I acknowledge that my primary loyalty is to Christ. We have no king but Jesus, and all of our national allegiance must be subordinate to the Kingdom of God.

In 2010 my focus, I believe from the Lord, became centered upon the dynamic ministry of Christ as described by John in the first chapter of his gospel. Due to the kindness of Pastors Gary and Gina Holley and The Fontana Christian Fellowship International church in Fontana, CA, I was given permission to preach my series of messages now written in this book.

My meditation, beginning in the later part of 2009 was on both the Twin Towers and what I now call the Twin Towers of the Father's revelation to us in Christ, grace and truth. Just as the twin towers in New York represented who we were and are as a nation, the twin towers of the Father's heart represent who we are in Christ.

The following is derived from my study and preaching on John 1:6-18, with special emphasis on verses 14-18. In these nine chapters, based upon my five messages, I hope to tantalize your taste buds and fully whet the appetite of you, the reader. I want to encourage you to get the CD's or DVD of the messages to go deeper in personal study on these Twin Towers of the Father's Heart...grace and truth. Discover not only who He is, but also who you are in Him.

Dr. Stan DeKoven

Introduction

For most of my life I have tried to find the balance, if there is such a thing, between grace and truth. In this book, grace and truth stand side by side with one another, not in contrast or competition. Grace, which will be defined in chapter one, is one of the most marvelous words known to man. Truth is not just another word, nor is it another religious concept. Truth is the embodiment of the thoughts and intents of God. It is an expression of the personhood of Christ for God's word tells us that he is the way, the truth, and the life. Grace and truth, in essence, are partners, working together to assist us as people to be everything God has already declared we are, but more on that later.

Truth knows no limits and no boundaries. God's ways are not man's ways nor can God's thoughts and intents be contained within the limitations of man's ability to understand. The vastness of God's truth is beyond human comprehension.

God is God and He will continue to be so for all of eternity. God does not change in His intentions or purposes, nor does His word. He is God and there is no other. God's truth is the sum total of all that He is and all that He shall ever be forever and ever. Who could hope to define God? Words are insufficient to accomplish such a task; however we do know one word that attempts to

Introduction

enlighten us to His nature, for the word says that He is love. So what is love and how does love express the nature of God? What can we hope to learn of God from love? Well, as we will explore, it is related to grace and truth.

If God is indeed the maker of Heaven and Earth (and we know that He is) then how does God's truth pave the way to living life fully, now and forever? Of course, the bible simply affirms that Jesus is the truth, but how do we relate to truth, recognizing that as humans we are almost constantly in violation of some aspect of truth, often suffering the consequences for not obeying the truth. In many ways, truth is, in that it is contained in all that Jesus Christ is... was... and is to come... the Almighty.[1]

Truth knows no end, it has no beginning. God's Truth attempts to define who God is, but the vastness of such a definition is too incalculable and too immense to be contained or comprehended by the mind of mortal man. However the spirit in a man can know who He is, at least in measure, if not in total. It is an experiential knowing, not one of the intellect alone.

Truth does not attempt to explain itself. It needs no explanation; it is not accountable to man. Nor is it accountable to nature. It simply is. God's grace makes it possible for us to live out His truth. Without God's grace we would be wholly unable to live a life in keeping with His desires.

Without His grace we would die separated eternally from God. While truth always affirms the authority and sovereignty of God, we know that God is infinitely merciful, and for those that know Him, he clothes us with His grace; what the bible calls a priestly garment of

---

[1] See: *The Overcomers Life*, Dr. Stan DeKoven, Vision Publishing, Ramona, CA

righteousness. It makes us acceptable before God, who has standards that we can only meet through His grace. When we repent of our sin, come into a correct relationship with the Lord, because of the wonderful grace of God provided through the death, burial and resurrection of Jesus Christ, we receive life.

Therefore we can stand before a Holy God, facing the Truth without condemnation or shame because of the garment that makes us acceptable and holy before Him. All of this is a work of Grace.

In the tabernacle of Moses we see a type of the plan of salvation, where the Ten Commandments are presented as the skeletal framework of truth. In reality, as Paul later states, the law reveals the harsh reality of divine authority and man's inability to live up to His expectation on his own. Jesus came as Truth in the flesh, that by grace we might be able to live with the law of God, which is His love written on our hearts. The tabernacle is where grace and truth abide side by side, in harmony with one another. Jesus Christ is that tabernacle.

The Truth, the Word, the law; what do these words have in common and what do they mean in terms of grace? And how does one define grace? Again, this will be clearly defined in the next chapter. One thing for certain is the word of God gives us ample indication of what the grace of God is, and what it does for us. David wrote of the grace of God that removes sin;

> "As far as the east is from the west, So far has He removed our transgressions from us." —Psalms 102:12

Paul echoes that the enormity of the love of God provided to us freely by Christ... the divine motivation for grace.

xv

Introduction

> "For I am convinced that neither death, nor life, nor angels, nor principalities, nor things present, nor things to come, nor powers, 39 nor height, nor depth, nor any other created thing, will be able to separate us from the love of God, which is in Christ Jesus our Lord." —Romans 8:38-39

The grace of God far exceeds the limitation of mercy. It includes the concept of His love and His unmerited favor.

So we see that God's grace, mercy, and truth knows no limits nor does His love. God is a limitless God that defies explanation or definition. He simply is. As He so aptly stated in regards to Moses question, He is simply the "I AM."

> "God said to Moses, "I AM WHO I AM;" and He said, "Thus you shall say to the sons of Israel, I AM has sent me to you."
> — Exodus 3:14 (NASB)

He is who He is, He will be who He will be, and He has chosen to pour out His grace and truth on all mankind in and through His son Jesus Christ.

Thanks for Grace!

> "Where would I be, if Jesus didn't love me, where would I be, if He didn't care... where would I be if He hadn't sacrificed His life, whoa but I'm glad, so glad He did."
> —Andre Crouch

Chapter 1

The Grace that Dwells with Us

Perhaps one of the most endearing hymns in Christendom is "Amazing Grace" by John Newton. The Wikipedia article on Newton states:

> ""Amazing Grace" is a Christian hymn written by the English poet and clergyman John Newton, (1725-1807), published in 1779." Its message was that forgiveness and redemption are possible regardless of the sins people commit, and that the soul can be delivered from despair through the mercy of God. "Amazing Grace" is one of the most recognizable songs in the English-speaking world.Newton wrote the words from his own personal experience. He grew up without any particular religious conviction, but his life's path was formed by a variety of twists and coincidences that were often put into motion by his recalcitrant insubordination. He was pressed into the Royal Navy and became a

sailor. Eventually, he became involved in the trading of slaves. One night a terrible storm battered his vessel so severely that he became frightened enough to call out to God for mercy, a moment that marked the beginning of his spiritual conversion. His career in slave trading lasted a few more years until he quit going to sea altogether. That is when he began studying theology."

Anyone who has experienced firsthand the amazing love and forgiveness of God through Christ, by the empowerment of the Holy Spirit, can truly declare that His grace is amazing. It is no doubt from this vantage point, which as a former son of Thunder and now fully converted to be a lover of Christ alone; John the apostle writes his gospel (truly good news). In the gospel of John in the first chapter we read:

> "There came a man sent from God, whose name was John. He came as a witness, to testify about the Light, so that all might believe through him. He was not the Light, but he came to testify about the Light.
> There was the true Light which, coming into the world, enlightens every man. He was in the world, and the world was made through Him, and the world did not know Him. 11He came to His own, and those who were His own did not receive Him.
> But as many as received Him, to them He gave the right to become children of God, even to those who believe in His name, who were born, not of blood nor of the will of the flesh nor of the will of man, but of God.

And the Word became flesh, and dwelt among us, and we saw His glory, glory as of the only begotten from the Father, full of grace and truth. John testified about Him and cried out, saying, "This was He of whom I said, ' He who comes after me has a higher rank than I, for He existed before me.'"

For of His fullness we have all received, and grace upon grace.

For the Law was given through Moses; grace and truth were realized through Jesus Christ.

No one has seen God at any time; the only begotten God who is in the bosom of the Father, He has explained Him."

— John 1:6-18

The words of John, the beloved disciple of Jesus, who literally heard the heartbeat of God (see John 13:25), presents a picture of God the Father who was virtually unknown to the Jews of that day. The people, guided by religious leaders, did not understand the heart of the Father towards us, and Jesus, who with intention and purpose, as written so intimately by John in this passage, came to reveal or manifest Grace and Truth. First, presented here is the grace of God and its importance for us all.

The Grace that Dwells

"And the Word became flesh, and dwelt among us, and we saw His glory, glory as of the only begotten from the Father, full of grace and truth." —John 1:14

The Grace that Dwells with Us

The Word dwelt among us... He was full of grace and truth. In Matthew 1:23 the prophet Isaiah was quoted. "Behold, the virgin shall be with child and shall bear a son, and they shall call His name Immanuel," which translated means, "God with us."

God himself came to dwell among us in the form of a baby, and that baby was full of grace and truth. That baby brought with Him the redemptive cure for sinful man that he might once again live in harmony with God. All that God ever wanted, from the very beginning, was an intimate relationship with man.

The relationship God desired was first seen in His relationship with Adam and Eve in the garden. Daily they walked and talked with God, communicating with Him on an intimate and personal basis. The grace that dwells with us speaks of the intimate relationship we are permitted to enjoy with the creator of the universe. But how can we have a relationship with deity? It is only because of this wonderful thing called grace. His grace was evident with the man and the woman in the garden; His grace was given from the beginning.

Another beautiful example of God's desire to dwell among His children can be found in Exodus 20. God told Moses to separate out the children of Israel so He could talk directly to them. In verse 19 we find the people, having heard the thundering of the voice of God on the mountain, respond in intense fear. The people demanded that Moses talk with God for them. They did not want to even come near to God because of their fear. God's desire to live among His people was rejected by the very people He wished to have relationship with. And so, God resorted to communication with them through an intercessor, Moses. This was never the perfect will or intention of the Lord.

God did not desire distance in relationship. He wanted a close one, an intimate one; but God's people were filled with fear. They were intimidated by His presence. He wanted a relationship with them, and as with all relationships, one built upon trust... their trust in Him as sovereign, as creator and sustainer of the universe, and as provider and protector for them. But they refused. They gave in to their fear, and withdrew from the Lord, placing Moses between themselves and God. It was that same fear that eventually caused them to err in disobedience at the edge of the Promised Land. Because they were unwilling to develop a genuine relationship with the Lord, they did not have the faith to believe Him and to boldly enter into the land of promise.

It is out of a genuine relationship that one can exercise faith or trust. Faith and trust in a relationship requires maturity for it to grow, and one can assume that the children of Israel were simply not mature enough for a healthy relationship. An intimate relationship takes us into greater depths and higher levels of understanding in the knowledge of the person we are relating to, including God. The bible states that the people perish for lack of knowledge. In order to advance in the Kingdom of God we must know who He is, for in so doing we come to understand who we are. An understanding of one's identity is crucial to the exercising of the authority that was freely given to us as His adopted children. As His children, we were made in His image and His likeness, that we might exercise dominion over all God created (Gen 2:26-28).

The desire of God to dwell among His people, to cultivate an intimate relationship with them, was the plan. In spite of the disobedience, and in spite of their sin, He still loved them. How could this be possible? It is only by God's grace.

The Grace that Dwells with Us

Grace is defined as God's unmerited favor. It goes beyond mercy (which was shown to the Old Testament saints) and speaks of being spared from the punishment for sin, no matter how well-earned and deserved by most men and women. Grace goes beyond mercy, as it speaks of the positive benefit of God's blessings, blessings that we do not deserve. Christ came to reveal the Father, and to fulfill the promise he made to Abraham, the friend of God, to be a blessing to all nations (people groups).

Of course as we shall see, grace and truth are to flow seamlessly with one another. They are not mutually exclusive, although in some ways they must be kept in dynamic tension with each other. Let's look at several scriptural insights into grace and the dwelling presence of God as found in the scripture.

In Exodus the 20th chapter, once again you see the people of God prepared to be a kingdom of priests. They had been separated (sanctified) for three days as the Lord had instructed Moses. He desired to meet with his people, for they were to be a "peculiar treasure" to God. So Moses did as he was instructed to do.

On the third day the people were prepared to meet with God near the Mount of Sinai. It is recorded that there was smoke and fire and the whole mountain quaked. Then the voice of the Lord thundered; they recoiled in fear. It was at this visitation of God that the Ten Commandments were given, etched on stone with the very hand of God.

The law standing alone is unforgivingly rigid, not being cushioned by God's grace. The law is the skeletal formation of Truth. As Paul the apostle stated, in Romans 7:12-13, though the law is good, the law was primarily designed to show us our sin. It never had the power to deliver us from sin, nor the power to help us live in right relationship with God. Without the grace of God, the law is judgmental and hard. The basis of Truth, which is the law, condemns man of sin. Without God's grace it is a death sentence for all people.

God wanted the grace found in his presence to accompany the reality of the law that exposes man's sin. He never wanted man to live by the law alone, but to experience the Truth found in the law coupled with the grace of His presence. The "grace that dwells" speaks of God walking and talking with His people.

In John 1:14 we read how the Lord tabernacled or dwelt with us. The word tabernacle refers to his physical tent or his flesh. He chose to become one of us in order to become one with us, in our joys and in our sorrows, in our pleasures and our pain. John also referred to previous tabernacles or tents, which were the primary places of worship. (Now our worship is not with tents or buildings, but in the Spirit with a person, that is, Christ by the Spirit).

In the Old Testament, there were three key tents or tabernacles that the readers of John's writing would directly relate to. They carried significant meaning for the readers... they were the tabernacles of Moses, David and Solomon's Temple. More about these three tabernacles will be presented in Chapter 2.

Important Consideration

There are times in life when things happen beyond our control; we often do not understand where God is in the midst of our circumstances. The death of a loved one, a business that suddenly goes belly up and all of one's assets are lost. It may be an illness or disease, a tragic accident. A loved one that gets caught in the trap of an addiction to drugs, alcohol, or worse; it is called life, and

The Grace that Dwells with Us

it happens. Unfortunately, we don't have all the answers but we do have with us One who knows, cares and walks with us through the most difficult of circumstances... His name is Jesus.

Paul recounts in Second Corinthians...

> "Because of the surpassing greatness of the revelations, for this reason, to keep me from exalting myself, there was given me a thorn in the flesh, a messenger of Satan to torment me—to keep me from exalting myself! 8Concerning this I implored the Lord three times that it might leave me. 9And He has said to me, "My grace is sufficient for you, for power is perfected in weakness."
>
> —2 Corinthians 12:7

God's grace is sufficient. No matter what dilemma we may be facing, no matter how difficult it may seem, we have this same assurance that Paul had. God's grace is sufficient for every single need.

Chapter 2

Moses: The Plan of Salvation

So, what was the plan? How did God plan to rescue sinful man from the reality of his sin and the consequences of his disobedience? God always has a plan, and coming into agreement with His plan is a key to our success in life. So what was/is His plan?

The word tells us that God does nothing but He reveals it to His prophets first. We can find time and time again, God revealing His plan through a man or woman, leading to action required for God's people. From the first animals sacrificed to cover Adam and Eve's sin, to the elaborate plan to preserve a remnant of mankind in the flood, God has always had a plan. In the case of Noah, a preacher of righteousness in his time, he took a choice few, protected by God in the ark of safety. He allowed them to ride high above the waves of God's judgment upon the earth, while keeping Noah and his family safe, along with all of the animals that had been chosen, two by two, to repopulate the earth.

Another dramatic picture of God's future grace for us is seen in the near sacrifice of Isaac by his father Abraham. A substitute was provided, a ram, and Isaac's life was spared. Of course, we must not forget in the ministry of Moses, the first Passover, as God spared the homes and all that lived in them. The doorposts were marked with the blood of the lambs, that His chosen people might be spared.

Further, we see God's hand of grace in hearing and answering Hanna's prayer (1 Sam.1:18), God's favor on Gideon and his 300 warriors (Ju.6:17), providing for Ruth a champion in Boaz (Ru. 2:2), Esther with Vashti (Es. 2:17), and many other bible characters.

One of the greatest examples of God's grace in the Old Testament can be seen in the life of Moses. This grace is alluded to in John 1, as the Tabernacle of Moses, and the Temple of Solomon, were both in the minds of the people that John would have written his gospel for.

God wanted to make His plan evident, so He instructed Moses to construct the tabernacle in the wilderness. It was a type and a shadow of the redemptive plan that God would use to free His people from the consequences of their sin. God had a plan, and He wanted to make His plan clear and concise before the people that He dearly loved; His beloved children.

In Exodus 25: 9 we read:

> "According to all that I am going to show you, as the pattern of the tabernacle and the pattern of all its furniture, just so you shall construct it."

Tabernacle means "tent," "place of dwelling" or "sanctuary." It was a sacred place where God chose to meet with His people, the Israelites, during the 40 years they wandered in the desert under Moses' leadership. It was the place where the leaders and people came together to worship and offer sacrifices.

The tabernacle was first erected in the wilderness exactly one year after the Passover, when the Israelites were freed from their Egyptian slavery (circa 1450 B.C.). It was a mobile tent with portable furniture that the people traveled with, and set up, wherever they pitched their camp. The tabernacle was set in the center of the camp, and the 12 tribes of Israel set their tents around it according to their tribe.

The detailed plans regarding the preparation and building of the tabernacle were revealed to Moses in the wilderness. He then gave the orders to the skilled craftsmen who were anointed for the task of building the tabernacle.

> "Then I will dwell among the Israelites and be their God. They will know that I am the Lord their God, who brought them out of Egypt so that I might dwell among them."
> —Exodus 29:45-46

And so God lived (appeared) among His people in the tabernacle in the wilderness. He appeared to them as a pillar of cloud over the tabernacle by day, and a pillar of fire by night, a manifestation of God's presence with them. Before the people would set out on their journey, the cloud would lift, giving them clear guidance and direction. This was a powerful visual statement indicating God's presence among them.

It was apparent that the people of God needed this visual evidence of His presence, for they lived by sight. When Moses ascended up Mount Sinai for 40 days, the people did not see or hear from him. Once again the people lived by sight alone, and not by faith. In the absence of Moses, who was their visual symbol of authority, they grew impatient. They gave their gold to Aaron. He in turn made them a golden calf and they began worshiping it in the place of God. The calf became the visual symbol of the presence of deity.

Over ten generations the people had been forced to work as slaves in Egypt. It finally took its toll on the children of Israel, causing the slave mentality to be indelibly etched into their minds. The Egyptian rulers of their past had been accustomed to making idols, and they foolishly followed suit.

This act of disobedience demonstrated their perceived need to follow and worship a God who was visually tangible. God's provision of a tabernacle built according the pattern of heaven, allowed the people to see and sense God's presence. It also allowed Moses the opportunity to meet with God in a concrete place and not disappear into the mountain where they could not see him.

The Significance of the Tabernacle: A Place of Presence or Authority... Heaven on Earth

The significance of the Tabernacle cannot be ignored in John's writing. I was recently reading N.T. Wright's book Simply Jesus, where he discusses the importance of Tabernacle language to the people of the day. In Wright's research he found that the Tabernacle, beginning with Moses through David, Solomon and even Herod's rebuilt version, represented if you will, heaven on earth, or the place where heaven could be experienced on earth. The Tabernacle, with all of its ceremonies and sacrifices, represented the presence of God, or the Kingdom on earth, and Jesus was clearly stating that the old Tabernacle, the Temple, was indeed coming down (which it did in 70AD,

The Significance of the Tabernacle

see Matt.24) to be replaced first by himself, the king of the Kingdom.

Indeed, Christ, via our faith in Him, becomes the place where the Kingdom dwells. It is where the Kingdom of God had come to earth, or heaven on earth, by the Holy Spirit. Now we, the Body of Christ, are heaven come to earth. We are the place of God's presence, the Kingdom having come so the will of God would be done on earth as it is in heaven. Thus, in Christ, and now in us, the original creation mandate of God, given to the man and woman in the garden (Gen 2:26) (to be fruitful and multiply and take dominion of the whole earth not each other) would be fulfilled, for now and eternally; God dwells with man. All this happened in the coming of Christ and was fulfilled in his death, burial and resurrection, and through the outpouring of Holy Spirit. It happened then, and continues to happen now, by grace, which allows us to walk in truth, which is Jesus.

The Tabernacle was more than just a place to meet with the people of God. All of the components of the tabernacle were a part of an intricate visual aid to illustrate God's relationship with His people. God required the people to be holy before Him and obedient to His word.

This requirement was not lost on Moses alone, but rather it was where obedience and holiness had to begin. This is the primary reason why absolute obedience to the blueprint that God had given to Moses had to be adhered to. God gave very specific instructions regarding every aspect of the tabernacle, both inside and out. Only the most skilled workers were called upon to do this work.

God gave Moses specific instructions for the building and the service of the tabernacle. He established clear rules for their worship. They were not intended to burden the people, but to show God's unquestionable authority and holiness.

For example, the anointing oil for the tabernacle and the incense for the altar of incense (made from God's own prescribed formulas of spices) were both declared holy by God. They could only be used for the purpose of the tabernacle and anyone else using the same formula for their own consumption would be cut off from Israel (Exodus 30:34-38). The special garments for the priests were holy. If these special garments were not worn when serving the Lord, the priest could die.

> "They shall be on Aaron and on his sons when they enter the tent of meeting, or when they approach the altar to minister in the holy place, so that they do not incur guilt and die. It shall be a statute forever to him and to his descendants after him."
> —Exodus 28:43

> **Detailed Plans for the Tabernacle of Moses**
>
> **God's instruction** for the building and worship in the tabernacle of Moses included detailed blueprints which were in part:
>
> - Specific measurements and detailed instruction for:
>   - The Gate
>   - Brazen Altar and the Tabernacle Sacrifices
>   - Laver (Basin)
>   - Menorah
>   - Table of Showbread
>   - Golden Altar of Incense
>   - Holy of Holies and the Veil
>   - Ark of the Covenant
> - The ingredients for the anointing oil.
> - Explicit details on the preparation of the priest's garments.

The Tabernacle: Presentation of God's Redemptive Plan

As we have already discussed in part, John wrote in the New Testament: "The Word became flesh and made His dwelling among us." (John 1:14) This word "dwelling" is the same word as "tabernacle" in the Old Testament. In other words, God came in living flesh to dwell or to tabernacle among His people. As He walked upon the earth and lived among the Jews, Jesus fulfilled the picture of the Old Testament tabernacle. The tabernacle was a prophetic projection of the Lord's redemptive plan for His people, and the concept of tabernacle was most familiar to the people of Jesus' time.

In brief, the tabernacle sacrifices point to Christ and His finished work on the cross. The Brazen Altar was where the lamb was sacrificed (Christ, the Lamb of God, slain from the foundations of the world), signifying the death of Christ for the salvation of the world.

It was the sacrifice to be made for man's sin. Sacrificing began as early as Adam, as an animal had to be slain to clothe him and Eve. We know that they found themselves naked (vulnerable), for the glory of God that they walked in was diminishing (in dying you will die). Therefore the covering of God was gone as well, so they had to be covered by the skins of animals.

It was the cost for sin, the blood of goats and bulls. It was the required sacrifice, although we know that it was not sufficient for all of time, for it had to be offered time and time again. It was not perfect, that which was perfect was yet to come.

At the Laver, symbolic washing was done by the priest. The application for believers today is that we are forgiven through Christ's work on the cross, and we are continually washed through His Word. In Romans 12:2 Paul prompted us to not be conformed to this world, but to have our minds renewed. It is through the washing of the water of the word (Eph.5:26) that renewal of the mind comes. We need to be washed daily in His Word. A person must be clean, with sin removed, before standing in the presence of the Lord (of course, this is accomplished fully through Jesus Christ).

The Holy of Holies is the place where the Lord dwelled between the Cherubim. It was the most holy place of all, and only the High Priest could enter there. He could enter once each year to make atonement for the people. Of course, now there is no barrier between the most holy place (Christ) and His people. The veil has been torn from top to bottom and the sacrifice given for all of eternity.

Like the priests in Moses' day, we must be clothed in the priestly garment. Christ is our righteousness, and we are clothed with this priestly garment by the Holy Spirit. We receive this, and then walk in this righteousness, imparted to us by faith, as we put off the old man and put on the new. We have donned the garment of righteousness, which is given by grace, when we enter relationship with God as the one new man, which is Jesus Christ. We were made acceptable and holy before a holy God because of Christ. Thus, we are able to come boldly before His throne, into His presence, as we are, having been made righteous and clean by His love, acceptable by His grace.

> "Therefore I urge you, brethren, by the mercies of God, to present your bodies a living and holy sacrifice, acceptable to God, which is your spiritual service of worship."
> —Romans 12:1

Chapter 3

David's Tent

A Pattern of Worship for Future Generations

The Tabernacle of David is the name given to the tent that King David set up on Mount Zion in Jerusalem to house the Ark of the Covenant. It was the center of a somewhat new order of worship. The sacrifices established under Moses were still in play, but in David's tent there appeared a more joyful worship, which stood in contrast, or perhaps added to the solemn worship of Moses' Tabernacle. Instead of the sacrifices of animals alone, the sacrifices offered in David's Tabernacle were the sacrifices of praise, joy and thanksgiving (Psalm 95:2,100:4, 141:2).

The Tabernacle of David style of worship, perhaps more than the Mosaic model, typifies worship in the Church today. The writer of Hebrews clarified for all that Jesus fulfilled the sacrificial system of the Old Covenant by His death on the cross (Hebrews 1:3, 7:27, 9:12, 9:24-28). The sacrifices made in the Church by the New Covenant priesthood (of course, that is who we are) are the sacrifices of praise, joy and thanksgiving (Hebrews 13:15, 1 Peter 2:9).

In addition to providing a new model or emphasis in worship in the Church, the Tabernacle of David points to the proclamation and authority of Christ through His Church, thus foreshadowing the priestly, kingly and prophetic ministries of the Church (Revelation 1:6, 5:10, 19:10, Acts 2:17, 1 Corinthians 14:1,3-5, 24-25, 29, 39).

The Tabernacle of David: A Present Application

The prophet Amos spoke of the future church, stating

> "In that day will I raise up the tabernacle of David that is fallen and close up the breaches thereof; and I will raise up his ruins, and I will build it as in the days of old."
> —Amos 9:11

This prophecy was interpreted by the leaders of the first century Church as being fulfilled in their day.

> "And after they had held their peace, James answered, saying, Men and brethren, hearken unto me: Simeon hath declared how God at the first did visit the Gentiles, to take out of them a people for his name. And to this agree the words of the prophets; as it is written, After this I will return, and will build again the tabernacle of David, which is fallen down; and I will build again the ruins thereof, and I will set it up: That the residue of men might seek after the Lord, and all the

Gentiles, upon whom my name is called, saith the Lord, who doeth all these things. Known unto God are all his works from the beginning of the world." —Acts 15:13-18

James quotes from Amos 9 to show that the salvation of the Gentiles is the fulfillment of Old Testament prophecy. The church was living during the time of the restoration of the Tabernacle of David. The Apostles knew that the Church, as the restored Tabernacle of David, was the place where Christ is worshiped. The result of the Church embracing Davidic worship included prophecy and authority, perhaps providing the atmosphere conducive for the resulting great harvest of souls.

What is Davidic Worship?

The phrase "Davidic worship" simply means worship in the spirit of the Tabernacle of David, that is, worship that is an act of the whole person, not just the intellect nor merely form and ritual (though tradition, form, ritual, remembrance is a ;part of all healthy worship). Worship in David's Tabernacle included singing, instrumental music, standing, kneeling, bowing, upraised hands, clapping and dancing. Davidic worship, or worship from a sincere and open heart, fulfills the command of Jesus to...

"Love the Lord your God with all your heart, all your soul, all your mind and all your strength" —Mark 12:30

Key Chapters Regarding the Tabernacle of David

The establishment of David's Tabernacle is described in 2 Samuel 6 and 1 Chronicles 13-16. From these passages we see that David prepared a place for the Ark (1 Chr. 15:1), the Levites sanctified themselves for their ministry (1 Chr. 15:14) which was to carry the Ark and minister to the Lord (1 Chr. 15:2). All Israel joined in the procession (1 Chr. 15:3) which was marked by joyful instrumental and vocal music (1 Chr. 15:16-21) and dancing (2 Sam. 6:14, 1 Chr. 15:29). Despite all of this, the celebration was not without its detractors (2 Sam. 6:16, 1 Chr. 15:29).

The majority of the Psalms were originally sung in David's Tabernacle. These songs, many written by David himself who was the sweet psalmist of Israel, were expressions of devotion and gratitude for all the Lord had done for the people under David's leadership. In addition, they describe the full range of human emotions revealed as the presence of God was experienced, from deepest despair to highest joy.

The righteous kings of Israel that followed David reestablished Davidic worship within the context of Temple worship. These revivals of Davidic worship paved the way for spiritual renewal and military victory. These times of revival and victory were under Solomon (2 Chr. 5-7) - 101 B.C., Jehoshaphat (2 Chr. 20) - 896 B.C., Joash (2 Chr. 23-24) - 835 B.C., Hezekiah (2 Chr. 29-30) - 726 B.C., Josiah (2 Chr. 35) - 623 B.C., Ezra (Ezra 3:10-13) - 536 B.C. and Nehemiah (Neh. 12:28-47) - 446 B.C.

The Old Testament prophecies that specifically mention the Tabernacle of David are Isaiah 16:5 and Amos

9:11-12. There are numerous additional prophecies concerning the coming of Messiah and His kingdom that refer to Zion, the mountain of the Lord, the glory of the Lord and other images that are obvious references to the Tabernacle of David. See especially Isaiah 2:2-5, Isaiah 9:2-7, Isaiah 35, Isaiah 40:1-5, Isaiah 60:1-3, Isaiah 61, Isaiah 62, Jeremiah 33:10-22, Micah 4:1-2, and Haggai 2:6-7.

The New Testament contains many quotes by Jesus and the Apostles from passages in the Psalms and the Prophetic books. Several of these quotes contain prophecies concerning the coming of Messiah, destined to reign on David's throne. In speaking of the incarnation, John writes that Jesus tabernacled among us (John 1:14). The Church is referred to as the temple of God (1 Cor. 3:16, Eph. 2:19-22). The Tabernacle of David is specifically mentioned in Acts 15:16-17 as being fulfilled by the Church.

Scriptures referring to Davidic worship are not limited to the Old Testament. The New Testament tells us to sing psalms, hymns and spiritual songs (Eph. 5:19, Col. 3:16), to sing in the spirit (1 Cor. 14:15), to lift up holy hands in prayer (1 Tim. 2:8) and to offer to God the sacrifice of praise (Heb. 13:15). The book of Revelation records scene after scene of heavenly worship that includes shouting (Rev. 19:1), "Hallelujahs" (Rev. 19:7), singing the new song (Rev. 5:9), and bowing (Rev. 4:10).

A Sign of the Last Days

The Bible refers to the time of the Old Covenant as the former days and the time of Messiah, the New Covenant era, as the latter days. The First century Christians understood that they were living in the last days, the age of

David's Tent

Messiah's kingdom. Jesus came to build His Church, to gather a people out of every nation to worship and serve Him. Jesus continues to build His Church, the restored Tabernacle of David, and we continue to live in the last days.

Solomon's Temple

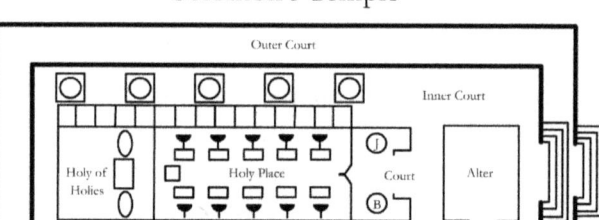

The above was adapted from principles presented by Bob Johnson, Zion Song Ministries

Chapter 4

The Temple of Solomon

In many ways, the Temple of Solomon was a demonstration of man's accomplishment, as he works in tandem with the purposes of God. Though the original dream of God was revealed to King David (2 Chronicles 28-29), it was left for Solomon to build, and build he did.

The crowning achievement of King Solomon's reign was the erection of the magnificent Temple (Beit ha-Mikdash) in Jerusalem. His father, King David, had wanted to build a House for God a generation earlier, as a permanent resting place for the Ark of God. However, God would not allow David to pursue his dream directly, waiting for a man of peace, that is Solomon, to accomplish the task. The fact is, blood flowed like water in David's kingdom, and God thought better of using his hands for the task of building a temple of peace and worship.

> "You will not build a house for my name," God said to him, "for you are a man of battles and have shed blood."
>
> —I Chronicles 28:3

The Temple of Solomon

The Bible's description of Solomon's Temple suggests that the inside ceiling was 180 feet long, 90 feet wide, and 50 feet high. The highest point in the Temple was actually 120 cubits tall (about 20 stories or about 207 feet).

According to the Tanach...

> "3:3 The length by cubits after the ancient measure was threescore cubits, and the breadth twenty cubits. 3:4 And the porch that was before the house, the length of it, according to the breadth of the house, was twenty cubits, and the height a hundred and twenty; and he overlaid it within with pure gold.
>
> Solomon spares no expense in the building's creation. He orders vast quantities of cedar from King Hiram of Tyre (I Kings 5:20-25), has huge blocks of the choicest stone quarried, and commands that the building's foundation be laid with hewn stone."
>
> —II Chronicles

To complete the massive project, he imposed forced labor on all of his subjects, drafting people for work shifts lasting a month at a time. Some 3,300 officials were appointed to oversee the Temple's erection (5:27-30). Solomon assumes such heavy debts in building the Temple that he is forced to pay off King Hiram with twenty towns in Galilee (I Kings 9:11).

When the Temple is completed, Solomon inaugurates it with prayer and sacrifice. He even invites non-Jews to come and pray there. He urges God to pay particular heed to their prayers:

"Thus all the peoples of the earth will know Your name and revere You, as does Your people Israel; and they will recognize that Your name is attached to this House that I have built." —I Kings 8:43

Until the Temple was destroyed by the Babylonians some four hundred years later, in 586 B.C.E, sacrifice was the predominant mode of divine service there. Seventy years later, a second Temple was built on the same site, and sacrifices again resumed. During the first century B.C.E., Herod greatly enlarged and expanded this Temple. The Second Temple was destroyed by the Romans in 70 C.E., after the failure of the Great Revolt.

As glorious and elaborate as the Temple was, its most important room contained almost no furniture at all. Known as the Holy of Holies (Kodes Kodashim), it housed the two tablets of the Ten Commandments. Unfortunately, the tablets disappeared when the Babylonians destroyed the Temple, and during the Second Temple era, the Holy of Holies was a small, entirely bare room. Only once a year, on Yom Kippur, the High Priest would enter this room and pray to God on Israel's behalf.

To this day, traditional Jews pray three times a day for the Temple's restoration. During the centuries the Muslims controlled Palestine, two mosques were built on the site of the Jewish Temple. (This was no coincidence; it is a common Islamic custom to build mosques on the sites of other people's holy places.) Since any attempt to level these mosques would lead to an international Muslim holy war (jihad) against Israel, the Temple cannot be rebuilt in the foreseeable future (and many theologians believe it will not likely ever be rebuilt, as the church is seen as the temple of God).[1]

Grace (Khane), even in the Old Testament, was a true virtue to be sought, knowing that God is good, all the time. In Ps. 84:11, the Psalmist states that God gives grace (favor) and glory to those who walk righteously (in truth). Also, grace comes by living obediently to godly instruction (Prov. 1:9). Grace is needed, and truth to live as God intends. Now we turn more specifically to the New Testament and the teachings of Christ and the apostles regarding grace and truth.

> "The law detects, grace alone conquers sin."
> — Saint Augustine of Hippo (354-430)[2]

Jesus: The Tabernacle of Grace and Truth Some Examples of Grace Personified

As significant as the three tabernacles are, which have been all too briefly discussed above, the tabernacle which matters most to our discussion is the One, Jesus the Messiah. Of course, there are so many examples of God's grace being manifested through the life of Christ during his earthly ministry. To follow are two that stand out, but first, another story about a different Grace.

---

[1] Source: Joseph Telushkin. Jewish Literacy. NY: William Morrow and Co., 1991.

[2] http://www.tentmaker.org/Quotes/grace_quotes.html

Grace Indeed

Her name just happened to be Grace, but she was anything but gracious in appearance or graceful in action. Tall, exceedingly thin and awkward, even her smile was more crooked than straight. But, ungraceful Grace was a woman full of grace - true grace she lived and grace she gave to others. She was an amazing woman.

I came to know Grace while pastoring a local church many years before. She introduced herself with her crooked smile and warm handshake, and in time I learned her remarkable story.

Born in Eastern Europe under communism, she suffered in extreme poverty. At 3 years of age she was abandoned by her mother (the father had left before her birth) to an orphanage, as the mother had no money to feed or cloth her. While in the orphanage, she suffered more deprivation and abuse until 11 years of age, when she was, as she stated many times, rescued by God, who used an American family for His purposes. Though a frightening change, she assumed that this would be the end of her suffering, but sadly no. In fact, she related that her adoptive mother was a lovely woman, but her marriage was unstable and home life unhappy. One bright spot, which she was always thankful for, was the fact that her new mom took her to church on a regular basis.

Within a year or so after the adoption, her adoptive father left the home, divorcing her mother, leaving mom and Grace to fend for themselves, but the mother was heartbroken and never really recovered from her loss, dying a short time later, leaving Grace alone again.

Hearing her story brought tears, and I expected her to be filled with anguish, bitterness and regret, but not Grace. In fact, she was more than philosophical. She was truly grateful, a key to result of a life filled with grace.

She was thankful to be alive, for she knew that, in spite of all that she had experienced, God and God's people, loved her. Yes, life was difficult and confusing at times, but she was convinced of God's love and grace, and was genuinely grateful for the gifts of an orphanage, a father, a mother and an opportunity, but most importantly, her real and most personal encounter with Jesus Christ. She truly experienced grace, and exuded grace to all she encountered.

An Important Parable of Two

When I first read the parable of the workers in the Vineyard, I was taken aback a bit. It did seem somewhat unfair that all workers no matter when they were hired (and thus how long they served or worked) were paid the same. This certainly did not seem to be the democratic thing to do. But of course, our sovereign God is not democratic but theocratic. In His kingdom He determines what is fair, and His grace is always lavish and seemingly unfair; but it is delightful, complete, and for His glory. Thus no matter when we come in or how much we serve, our rewards are the same. We obtain eternal presence with the Lord, eternal blessings from Him, and an eternal life flowing from His eternal well of love.

The story of the Father and the Prodigal is classic. In brief summary: a father, representing the Lord of course, a father of considerable wealth had two sons. The younger, against all protocol of the day, asked for his inheritance early. He then took off to a foreign country and squandered his wealth.

In time there was a famine, and no one was willing to help him. There was a lack of appropriate work, and as a Jewish boy he was obviously not prepared to work a pig farm. As a result of his own personal choices, he was in dire circumstances. He determined in his heart to return to his father, not as a son, but as a servant. Perhaps he felt unworthy because he had cared less for his father and more about the father's provisions. When he does finally get home, he is welcomed unconditionally. He was protected by the father and loved for who he was, not for what he could do. What a picture of the grace of God.

The attitude of the elder brother was typical of many in the church today. Unlike his (seemingly) unworthy brother, he felt that he deserved the father's wealth and a party as well. He had been both loyal and faithful. Didn't that count for anything? Certainly it counted, but not in terms of our salvation. As we readily acknowledge, faith and grace are essential. Ephesians 2:8, 9 "for by grace we are saved through faith (which is also a gift), and it is not of works." Works will no doubt follow our wonderful grace filled relationship with a Father who loves us, but no amount of works will save us or keep us saved.

Our salvation which is all by grace, provides for us multiple benefits. Those include healing, restoration of loss, eternity, and a purpose to live. It also includes a life abundant in blessings, flowing from the throne of God to the heart of every man who will receive his grace. (John 10:10) His grace is immeasurable to all who believe. We should be forever grateful.

An Application

Shortly after the assassination of President John Kennedy my mom gave her heart to the Lord (in her normal, dramatic style... going to the "altar" before allowing the poor preacher to even give the invitation.) This began a change in everything in my family. My mom suffered many a malady in life, some brought on by her own Irish temper, and some by multiple abuse situations. One thing was clear in regards to her experience with Christ. She loved Jesus, for he first loved her.

I think this must be a most important launching point for all believers, to really know, not intellectually but to the depths of one's soul, that Jesus loves us. We have the privilege to love him. Grace was a reality for my mother, complicated as she was at times. She received the Lord's forgiveness for the past, the present and the future. It was the transforming substance of her life.

She, unlike many other believers of her time (and of today) never forgot where she came from, who saved her, and how undeserving she was. She was grateful on a daily basis that the God of the universe had chosen her to be a member of His family. I am convinced that as she pushes her way to the head of the line to see Jesus in heaven, she continues to rejoice a bit louder than most. Someday, because of His grace, perhaps the whole family will join in the throng.

In conclusion, here are some final thoughts on the four tabernacles or tents of God's grace dwelling with us:

1. In the tabernacle of Moses we could see the plan for salvation. It was God's grace to reunite His children to Himself.

2. In the Tabernacle of David we see David modeling worship for the future church and proclaiming the authority of Christ, helping to fulfill the church to exhibit the Lord's Priestly, Kingly, and Prophetic ministries within the church. This tabernacle was to be rebuilt and restored in the New Covenant, a covenant open to Jew and Gentile alike, fulfilling the promise to Abraham.

An Application

3. Solomon's temple in all of its splendor and glory not unlike the bride of Christ today, being adorned as a house of glory for the one and only God, and in service to Him.

4. Finally, the tabernacle of God with us, Jesus himself, who was filled with Holy Spirit without measure, which was broken by a Roman crucifixion, opening the door for men and women like us to experience His grace, and become a part of the continuing tabernacle of God in the earth, the church.

Each of these personified the Christ that came to dwell among His people. Grace, a free gift from God to His people, simply because He loved them and wanted to dwell with them, is God's greatest achievement. Grace made the intimate relationship of God with His people possible.

A Quote on Glory:

> "A man can no more diminish God's glory by refusing to worship Him than a lunatic can put out the sun by scribbling the word, 'darkness' on the walls of his cell."
> —C.S. Lewis[3]

---

[3] *The Problem of Pain,* http://www.quotegarden.com/god.html

Chapter 5

The Grace that Manifests the Father's Glory

What does it mean to manifest the glory?

One cannot manifest that which they do not have. Unless you have accepted the saving grace of God through the gift of His son, you cannot manifest the glory of God. You must have it, to manifest it. Those who have come to the saving knowledge of the Son and have accepted his provision for their sins, have the glory of God residing within them. It is the grace of God that has made this provision available to each of us.

It is this saving grace that makes the glory of God an element of our renewed nature. It is the nature and glory of God birthed in us, as a result of our salvation experience. Although we have this glory birthed within us, it is up to us to allow that new nature to manifest itself within our lives.

This gift of grace upon our lives is freely given, but it is not to be selfishly kept to ourselves. 1 Corinthians 12:7 "but to each one is given the manifestation of the Spirit for the common good." It is for all of the body of Christ to enjoy and be edified through the gift of grace that has been given. The gift of grace has been given to each individual in a measure, so that when we come together as His church, we can share the gifts given with each other, and the world.

Jesus' purpose was to reveal the Father to a world who did not understand Him. His name, as mentioned to Moses, is I Am that I Am, or I will be what I will be, and he is calling us to be what we were meant to be, to live in His glory.

Revealing the Father - Old Testament

The grace that manifests the Father's Glory in the Old Testament, called the Shekinah glory speaks of the weight, the splendor, and the honor which justly belongs to God and God alone. Much has been taught of late on the glory of God. The hunger to experience God's glory, mostly seen in the more charismatic wing of the church of Christ, is not a new pursuit. From the earliest of God's dealings with his creation (see the Garden story) His glory or presence has been man's pursuit.

Perhaps the most noteworthy of the Old Testament leaders to openly seek the glory or presence of God was the Prophet Moses. In the book of Exodus, Chapter 33 we read:

> "And he said unto him, If thy presence go not with me, carry us not up hence: For

wherein shall it be known here that I and thy people have found grace in thy sight? Is it not in that thou goest with us? So shall we be separated, I and thy people, from all the people that are upon the face of the earth.

And the LORD said unto Moses, I will do this thing also that thou hast spoken: for thou hast found grace in my sight, and I know thee by name. And he said, I beseech thee, shew me thy glory.

And he said, I will make all my goodness pass before thee, and I will proclaim the name of the LORD before thee; and will be gracious to whom I will be gracious, and will shew mercy on whom I will show mercy. And he said, Thou canst not see my face: for there shall no man see me, and live.

And the LORD said, Behold, there is a place by me, and thou shalt stand upon a rock: And it shall come to pass, while my glory passeth by, that I will put thee in a cleft of the rock, and will cover thee with my hand while I pass by: And I will take away mine hand, and thou shalt see my back parts: but my face shall not be seen."
—Exodus 33:15-23

Ex 33:15-23 speaks of his glory as His grace, compassion, goodness, His Face, for He indeed is the King of Glory. Christ is mighty and strong, and worthy of praise. Through the grace or by the grace of God the Lord manifests His presence. In the Old Testament He manifested himself in theophanies, in demonstrations of power (Plaques, Red sea, Pillar of fire and Cloud) and through His word via the 10 Commandments in His own hand and via the prophets.

The Father Revealed from Old to New Testament

As glorious as God's presence was in the Old Testament, nothing compares to His self-revelation through His own son Jesus Christ. As we have previously read, John 1: 14-16 reads:

> "And the Word was made flesh, and dwelt among us, (and we beheld his glory, the glory as of the only begotten of the Father,) full of grace and truth. John bare witness of him, and cried, saying, This was he of whom I spake, He that cometh after me is preferred before me: for he was before me. And of his fulness have all we received, and grace for grace."

As stated above, the Glory of God has been a pursuit since the earliest of times. We mentioned a few, but the topic deserves a deeper look. For example, in Exodus 16:7 Manna was a manifestation of His glory (presence). Manna was a perfect food, which provided complete balance to the children of Israel's diet, providing them health and vitality during their time of sojourning in the Wilderness.

Of course, once it was time to move into the land of promise, a walk of faith would be required, sans Manna, The Pillar of Fire or the Cloud to protect them from the heat of the sun. Maturity requires faith.

In Psalms 24:7, Jesus is referred to as the King of Glory. Christ, mighty and strong, the one we lift up, though humbled in the flesh, would and does reign eternally, the King of kings, and the Lord of lords.

New Testament Revelation of the Father

Further in the vision of God was to see the entire earth filled with the knowledge (dah'ath, means cunning, knowledge, and awareness) of the glory of the Lord. His presence was to be manifested everywhere as the waters cover the sea (or everywhere).

The fact is that sinners fall short of His glory (Romans 3:23). We know that all fall short, but we are no longer just sinners saved by grace. We are sons, even more than sons we are friends, inheritors, and joint heirs with Christ. Thus, the gospel of the Glory of Christ is what we preach (2 Co 4:4). The Greek word in this case is Doxa, meaning honor or praise. So we sing: Praise God from whom all blessings flow, praise Him all creatures here below, praise Him above ye heavenly host, praise Father, Son and Holy Ghost. Amen!

Learning to Share

Ultimate glory, the presence and power of Christ in and through the Holy Spirit, is to be shared. This was the decision of the Father and the Son as presented in Jesus' High Priestly prayer in John 17:1-12, 22-23):

> "These things Jesus spoke, and lifting up
> His eyes to heaven, He said, Father, the hour

The Grace that Manifests the Father's Glory

has come; glorify thy son, that the son may glorify Thee, even as Thou gavest me authority over all mankind, that to all whom Thou has given Him, He may give eternal life

And this is eternal life, that they may know Thee, the only true God and Jesus Christ whom Thou hast sent. I glorified Thee on the earth, having accomplished the works which Thou has given me to do. And now glorify Thou me together with Thyself, Father, with the glory which I had with Thee before the world was. I manifested Thy name to the men whom Thou gavest Me out of the world; Thine they were, and Thou gavest them to Me, and they have kept Thy word.

Now they have come to know that everything Thou hast given Me is from Thee; for the works which thou gavest me I have given to them and they received them and truly understood that I came forth from Thee, and they believed that Thou didst send me.

I ask on their behalf; I do not ask on behalf of the world, but for those whom Thou hast given Me; for they are Thine; and all things that are Mine are Thine, and Thine are Mine; and I have been glorified in them. While I was with them, I was keeping them in Thy name which Thou hast given Me; and I guarded them, and not one of them perished but the son of perdition, that the Scripture might be fulfilled ...

And the glory which Thou hast given Me I have given to them; that they may be one, just as We are one; I in them, and Thou in Me, that they may be perfected in unity, that

> the world may know that Thou didst send me and didst love them, even as Thou didst love Me." —John 17:1-12, 22-23

In My house there are many rooms I have gone to make a place for you. In My body there are many members, each has their place (room) in the body. Each is significant, each in their own way, from the greatest to the least. All are equally important in God's eyes and significant to the body of Christ. We are only truly whole as we come together in unity.

It is as each member of the body of Christ, each room in His House, each earthen vessel allows the light of His glorious gospel to shine from the inside. that we can begin to fill the whole earth with His glory. It is a progressive act, as we have revelation within ourselves and allow the light of His word to change us; we begin to glow brighter and brighter each day. It is this illumination of Jesus through the Holy Spirit abiding in us that reveals His glory. From glory to glory, we see the light shine. As the body grows and matures, the glory intensifies advancing His Kingdom.

Both now and for all of eternity, grace received and walked in by faith, is shared between the Father, Son and Holy Spirit, as well as the Bride of Christ, the church. What a grace we share!

Another Quote:

> "Everyone can be great because anyone can serve. You don't have to have a college degree to serve. You don't even have to make your subject and verb agree to serve... You only need a heart full of grace, a soul generated by love." —Martin Luther King, Jr.[1]

---

[1] http://www.joyofquotes.com/index.html

Chapter 6

The Grace Upon Grace for Us

> "Just as a father has compassion on his children, so the LORD has compassion on those who fear Him. For He Himself knows our frame; He is mindful that we are but dust." —Psalm 103:13-14

What Price Must You Pay for His Grace?

What price indeed? I suppose the most radical and delightful aspects of grace, is its freeness. How risky for God to put all of His eggs in this one basket. It was for our sakes, because God saw how much we needed His grace. "He is mindful that we are but dust." He knew what He had made us from. He knew of the weakness we had in our earthen bodies, and He made provision for it in His Son.

John 1:16, grace upon grace is a phrase used by John the apostle. It was for the sake of grace that God, in His divine foreknowledge owned the problem of sin. It was not that He caused sin, but though innocent of the cause or consequences, he nonetheless provided the remedy.

His great love was demonstrated by His great sacrifice. When one thinks about God's grace for us and grace upon us, we will often sense the plenteousness or fullness of the redemption provided by our God. Through His grace in Christ, God was bringing us back to Himself for God's own purposes. Because of His mercy and dynamic love it is possible for us to forgive and to give, both mercy and grace.

His grace was free to each who would receive. It was Christ who paid the price, not us. It was freely given and may be freely received. How do we acknowledge an over the top, exceedingly abundant kind of God? What do we owe Him in exchange for His grace? We know that he puts no price on His grace; it really is free. Yet we owe him all that we are and all that we shall ever be in Him. So how can we, as His loving children, reciprocate such a great act of unselfish love?

Perhaps Paul said it best in Romans12:1

> "Therefore I urge you, brethren, by the mercies of God, to present your bodies a living and holy sacrifice, acceptable to God, which is your spiritual service of worship."

Because He has saved us through His grace, we owe Him our lives. We demonstrate our gratitude to Him by sacrificing our own bodies (including our mind, will, and emotions) to worship Him. The first and greatest commandment is to love the Lord, but the second is to love our neighbor. I am not at all certain that we can do either, without His grace, nor can we neglect one for the other. As His children, we show our love by demonstrating that love for Him in worship, and secondly by

What Price Must You Pay for His Grace?

the fulfilling of His commandments. Yet, even if we do not keep His commandment to love (in fact, who really can), He still loves us, forgives us, helps us, empowers us. What grace!

As believers we are empowered by the Lord to also demonstrate actions of grace to others; grace livers and grace givers we can be. Living a life of grace, showing favor to others as we need favor for ourselves, we live the purposeful life God intended.

What was it that Peter asked of Jesus in Matthew 18:21?

> "Then Peter came and said to Him, "Lord, how often shall my brother sin against me and I forgive him?" Up to seven times? 22 Jesus said to him, "I do not say to you, up to seven times, but up to seventy times seven."

We demonstrate our love for our Father as we show love and forgiveness to one another.

> "Be kind to one another, tender-hearted, forgiving each other, just as God in Christ also has forgiven you." —Ephesians 4:32

His grace makes it possible even in the most difficult of circumstances. It enables us to not take revenge when revenge would feel so sweet. It empowers us to turn the other cheek, when smacking the person who smacked us, would be most satisfying. It gives us the strength to humble ourselves, to the point of praying for those who despitefully use us and even hate us, and we do it for the sake of His name.

Thus, we receive grace to communicate grace, with our actions and our words, beginning with our most intimate friends and family. Little by little to all within our sphere of influence, we share the grace so freely given. Of course, we can't give if we have not received.

Remember in the Old Testament, although grace was there, it was not understood. Mercy was ample for God's people. Grace in the New Testament is now fulfilled through the grace of Christ. When Jesus declared on the cross that "It is finished", it meant that he had poured out his physical life for all mankind. In the release of the Holy Spirit, the door was open for the grace in us to answer the grace in Him. This is achieved in our worship and service, which is not mandatory for us to receive God's grace but will naturally flow from us to others because of His grace.

This remarkable mutual response of grace and mercy to others, mutual admiration for our fellow strugglers, and to live out the grace filled life, is beyond our old nature for certain. This is demonstrated by the mutual submission in relationships both in and out of the church. Most importantly, it is led by submission to the Lordship of Christ.

His Grace, Our Graciousness

There are several other scriptures that speak about grace in relationship to us as believers. In Romans 1:5 Paul the apostle states;"through whom we have received grace and apostleship to bring about the obedience of faith among all the Gentiles, for His name's sake."

It is precisely through the grace of God in Christ that we are able to live a life of obedience to the word of God. We are saved by grace, and we remain saved, if you will, by grace, which produces works of obedience from us. Our works, good works for the benefit of others, remains the clearest sign that one is walking in relationship with the Lord. A similar statement is made by Paul in Romans 5:2.

Further, we know that the Lord is our provider, who gives us what we need by grace. In 2 Corinthians 9:8, 9 we read;

> "And God is able to make all grace abound to you, that always having all sufficiency in everything you may have an abundance for every good deed; as it is written, He Scattered Abroad, He Gave to the Poor, His Righteousness Abides Forever."

Of course, His grace to provide for us is predicated on our graciousness...in this case, our graciousness in giving. First, the Lord wants us to give our hearts, then our finances to support the work of the Lord, and to care for the poor. We remember that we have received by grace all that we need and in most cases in abundance. We need to be generous in our time, talent and treasure, which should flow from the abundance of a grace filled heart.

> "Bless the Lord, Oh my soul, and forget not all His benefits (which frankly, we often do), but wow, what benefits, what glory, and what a wonderful savior is Jesus our Lord. How can we forget? Help me not to forget."
> —Many a Believer

Chapter 7

The Grace of Truth for Us: Truth or Consequences

As previously stated in the Old Testament, the Law of Moses was in fact full of mercy and grace, as God was gracious to His people, the children of Israel. He gave them such wonderful benefits, especially compared to other nations in their region of the world. This includes (not a comprehensive list):

The Word or Law

To govern them, which was not unheard of by other nations, for many nations had laws to follow, but all such word, was backed by an earthly deity, a Pharaoh or King. We know that the Ten Commandments were given to Moses and etched upon stone, a type and foreshadow of the day when the law would be written upon the table of our hearts. We are living epistles.

The Word of God

The law to govern His people, was, as described by King David, truly perfect.

The Grace of Truth for Us: Truth or Consequences

> "The law of the Lord is perfect, restoring the soul; The testimony of the Lord is sure, making wise the simple. The precepts of the Lord are right, rejoicing the heart; The commandment of the Lord is pure, enlightening the eyes. The fear of the Lord is clean, enduring forever; The judgments of the Lord are true; they are righteous all together. They are more desirable than gold, yes, than much fine gold, Sweeter also than honey and the drippings of the honeycomb." —Ps. 19:7-10

The Promise of Success and Prosperity

The word of God had the power to make them powerful, successful, and prosperous. See the instruction given to Joshua.

> "Only be strong and very courageous; be careful to do according to all the law which Moses My servant commanded you; do not turn from it to the right or to the left, so that you may have success wherever you go. 8"This book of the law shall not depart from your mouth, but you shall meditate on it day and night, so that you may be careful to do according to all that is written in it; for then you will make your way prosperous, and then you will have success. 9"Have I not commanded you? Be strong and courageous! Do not tremble or be dismayed, for the LORD your God is with you wherever you go."
> —Joshua 1:7

Again in Psalms 1 we see:

"How blessed is the man who does not walk in the counsel of the wicked, Nor stand in the path of sinners, Nor sit in the seat of scoffers!

But his delight is in the law of the LORD, And in His law he meditates day and night.

He will be like a tree firmly planted by streams of water, Which yields its fruit in its season And its leaf does not wither; And in whatever he does, he prospers."

—Psalms 1:1-3

The Promise of Protection

Further, God provided to the children of Israel, His chosen, protection in the wilderness; the cloud by day to protect them from the sun, the pillar of fire by night to ward off fear, and the Manna from heaven that fed them. These miraculous provisions were grace for the people as they journeyed in the wilderness. Of course, one must be careful to not over generalize any promise of God, as they were, in many cases, specific to the day and time, and also, often exaggerated (using the concept of hyperbole) to emphasize the important point being made.

The Promise of Provision

Also, God provided leaders to help them, including Moses, Joshua, Aaron, Miriam, and eventually others, with the greatest leaders being Moses and David. Of course, none of these leaders were perfect, but were chosen and anointed to assist the people to stay on task. Even though they seemed to resist at every turn, God continued to provide key leaders to guide and care for them, even as God would.

The Promise of His presence

The Grace of Truth for Us: Truth or Consequences

Along with key leaders, God himself walked with His people, showing patience in His longsuffering journey with them, and significant mercy to rescue them, even after He divorced them to marry another (the New Covenant church, consisting of Jew and Gentile) He continued to reconcile them because He simply loved them, chose them and watched over them.

In His Will

Grace presented God's will concerning man and His good will towards us, but it was also fearful and dutiful. It was clear that to follow God and to fear Him was really not an option for the people of God. Yet in Christ, as we have previously stated, we have grace and truth. In fact, in Christ grace goes beyond that of Moses, for it provided what Moses or the law could not; for we were:

- Cleansed; not just covered in our sin, but legitimately and fully cleansed from our sin nature, set free from the power of sin and death, translated from the kingdom of darkness to the Kingdom of His own dear Son. The fact is, the issue was never becoming good enough for God; that is an impossible task, or of being too bad for redemption. The issue has always been life or death. For Christ translates from death to life by the power of His shed blood and resurrection. Further, we have been...

- Delivered from our sin, and the consequences of sin, and from the dominion of Satan and his minions. What a full salvation we have received, what grace; what blessings in Jesus. Also, we have been....

- Freed to be all He created us to be, and, as stated above, to share the same grace with others, which leads us to the importance of ...

Truth or Consequences

The fact is, grace does not remove consequences for our decisions and misdeeds for the scripture still states that seed time and harvest or sowing and reaping would never cease (Gen. 8:22). We can, however, walk in truth by grace, as empowered by the Holy Spirit. We can avoid experiencing the ultimate outcome of sin, no matter how well deserved, as a result of this gift we call grace.

Again, truth is a twin of grace and is defined as:

- Fidelity, constancy, sincerity in action, character and utterance, the state of being the case, fact... a transcendent fundamental or spiritual reality; the body of true statements and propositions. In truth: in accordance with fact or actually, we see demonstrated by attitude and action, such as in...

- Joshua 24:14, as in sincerity the children of Israel were to put away idols, and though they struggled with this issue their whole journey with the Lord, it was always God's desire that they walk away from idols, and embrace the Word of God in fullness.

- In I Kings 2:4, the word states that they were to follow the Lord with all their heart. If they did so, He would always provide leadership capable of leading them in truth and towards truth.

Of course, according to Ps 25:5, 10, and 51:6, truth must be taught — and God's people must be lead; God calls leaders and followers to keep covenant with Him. That was always the challenge for God's people, and the failure to remain in covenant with the Lord led to all the difficulties throughout the Old Testament history.

Get in the Flow

Remember, it is not just grace and kindness, or truth and righteous, but it is both grace and truth, flowing together that makes for our balanced and effective life in Christ (Proverbs 3:3). This Old Testament principle is echoed over and over in the New. It is seen in John 8:32, 14:6, 18:37, 38. The Word abides, so we must know and apply the truth. This leads to true freedom when we follow fully the One who is truth, for Jesus is Truth.

There is a song I remember so well from my childhood, "There Is a Fountain Filled with Blood" written by William Cowper, 1731-1800, that speaks of the fountain that washes away the guilty stains or the results of sin in our lives. It is the blood of Jesus that washes us clean as snow, by God's grace. We need to get in the flow and allow His grace balanced by His Truth to lead us into the paths of righteousness.

This awareness should lead us to renounce former ways of behaving that do not line up with God's word, and embrace the truth of God's word (2 Cor. 4:2.) This includes putting off of the old and putting on of the new, renewing our minds, and putting on the new self as described in wonderful detail in Paul's writing, as well as James (Ephesians 4, Colossians 2, James 1, and Hebrews 12).

Most believers today are interested in, and desperately in need of grace. They desire to live a grace filled life, counting on the forever forgiving grace of our Father. They may often think of God more as a doting grandfather than Father, but God is our Father, providing abundant love and care, mixed with a healthy dose of discipline as needed. Most believers, especially young ones, struggle to live the principles of a Christian life (truth). It is not a relative truth but is demonstratively

Get in the Flow

stated in the Bible for our benefit; Grace and truth -both are needed, and in healthy measure. Thank God, our Father, through his Son, has fully provided to us all that is needed for life and godliness - through Christ.

> "Truth, you want the truth?
> ...I think I have a right...you can't handle the truth![1] "

---

[1] From scene between Tom Cruise and Jack Nicholson in *A few good men*, Columbia Pictures, 1992

Chapter 8

Results of Grace and Truth: Freedom and Transformation

We have all seen them, at times we have even been taken in by them; but the truth can be known if we watch for the fruit. Some may tell you they are Christians, they may act the part, dress the part, and may even know how to speak the part (fluent in the Christianese language), but the truth is proven by the fruit. What kind of fruit are they bearing at home away from the careful eye of the Christian community? What kind of fruit are they bearing when they are at work or attending a football game?

 Some can put on airs for a season, but the true fruit of repentance will make itself evident in due time. The true fruit of grace and truth will be evidenced by the life of one who has been truly transformed from the inside out.

 There are two key scriptures that speak of the results of grace and truth, or if you will, the evidence of a transformed life. First, we will look at Paul's letter to his son

Results of Grace and Truth

in the Lord, Timothy from I Tim 1:1-5."Paul, an apostle of Christ Jesus according to the commandment of God our Savior, and of Christ Jesus, who is our hope; to Timothy, my true child in the faith: Grace, mercy and peace from God the Father and Christ Jesus our Lord. As I urged you upon my departure for Macedonia, remain on at Ephesus, in order that you may instruct certain men not to teach strange doctrines, nor to pay attention to myths and endless genealogies, which give rise to mere speculation rather than furthering the administration of God which is by faith. But the goal of our instruction is love from a pure heart and a good conscience and a sincere faith."

As I have written more extensively in my book, "Transferring the Vision" Paul writes this personal and intimate letter to his son in the Lord, Timothy. He reminds him, no doubt based upon previous teaching, that the goal of the teaching ministry is transformation. Seeing true change come to a person from the inside out is transformation, made available to each of us by the gift of grace. Grace is the gifting of God, in this case given through the Five Fold ministry gift of the apostle/teacher. The goal of any teaching or training is change, growth, or maturity, as demonstrated by a change in the heart, mind and behavior of the recipient of the teaching.

The goal of grace and truth was for a disciple of Christ to grow in:

- Love (Agape), which meant both a change in affection and orientation, from self to God and His purposes, and also from selfish ambition to compassion, or love that is acted upon.

- Perception or Thinking. Along with a change in the heart of a person, there should also be a change of thinking, which is what Paul calls a good conscience. This comes from a purified heart, one cleansed by the blood of Jesus Christ, and by the washing of the water of the word. A good conscience is essentially a God consciousness, having the mind of Christ. This develops as we repent (change our thinking from the world to Christ and His word) and believe what the word of God says to us in our daily walk with Him.

- Behavior or Lifestyle. Finally, there should be an outworking of faith, which is a change of behavior. Paul calls this a sincere faith. Another way of stating this is that a believer exposed to the word of God, over time, should change from the inside out. His heart first, then his thought process, and then behavior.

Much of church history has focused on external change which is important, but should be the result of inward change, not in place of it.

Being Who You Already Are

Another way of discussing the results of Grace and Truth applied to our lives can be seen in Paul's writings to the church in Colossians.

> "For in Him all the fullness of Deity dwells in bodily form, and in Him you have been made complete, and He is the head over all rule and authority; and in Him you were also circumcised with a circumcision made without hands, in the removal of the body of the flesh by the circumcision of Christ; having

been buried with Him in baptism, in which you were also raised up with Him through faith in the working of God who raised Him from the dead; And when you were dead in your transgressions and the uncircumcision of your flesh" —Colossians 2:9-15

He made you alive together with Him, having forgiven us all our transgressions, having cancelled out the certificate of debt consisting of decrees against us and which was hostile to us; and He has taken it out of the way, having nailed it to the cross. When He had disarmed the rulers and authorities He made public display of them, having triumphed over them through Him." (Notice the author's emphasis.)

Please note the tense of Paul's writing. It is past tense, the significance of which is enormous for the believer. Because of all Christ has done for us, having our sin nailed to the cross on our behalf, we now can live full and gloriously free from the guilt and shame of the past. We can walk in victory through the empowerment of the Spirit in us. This truth is difficult for many believers to grasp.

If fully comprehended, this reality leads us to being who we already are; free, cleansed, forgiven, loved, and graced! All of these benefits are given to us. It then flows from a shared life, for we must remember we share this together, not just individually. It helps to remember Christ is in us, and He is the hope of glory. (Col 1:27)

Because He lives in us by grace, as we walk in truth, we can live a balanced life, (Luke 2:52). This balanced life was essential for our Lord Jesus, who grew in wisdom and knowledge and in favor (grace) with God and man. As He grew, so can we naturally grow, by His grace lived out in truth. For He has called each of us to live fully with a...

- Kingdom Perspective (Rom 14:17), where our focus is always on living right (we have been made righteous, and now must live right as He gives us strength), walking in peace (Christ is our peace, and we can live at peace in the midst of any storm) while filled with the joy of the Lord, which is our strength. In other words, we can grow in:

- Freedom and Maturity, going beyond childhood and adolescence to maturity or fatherhood is truly possible. As John Grubb stated in his teachings in Japan, "Fatherhood has forgotten his own growth, is free from his own concerns, and is occupied in service to others. God doesn't live for Himself. God is the everlasting servant of His own creation in infinite grace, and in an endless stream for self-giving. In His infinite grace He is concerned about us. And so, to know Him, that is from the beginning, is to have His exact character, and to have that by nature (our new nature in Christ)."[1]

In Christ, we are (now) new creations, the old things have (past tense) passed away, behold all things (in Christ and in us) are new (2 Cor. 5:17). The goal in the Christian life, and the difficulty for most of us, is walking out what we have already received in and through the death and resurrection of Jesus Christ. With God's grace, and as we walk in truth, all things are possible — if we believe.

---

[1] For more on this, see 1 John 2:12-14 and my book, Journey to Wholeness.

Results of Grace and Truth

"Faith is the strength by which a shattered world shall emerge into the light."—Helen Keller[2]

---

[2]http://www.joyofquotes.com/faith_quotes.html

Chapter 9

Grace and Truth: We Can't Live Without Them

Grace and truth represent the fullness of who God (Father, Son and Holy Spirit) is. As the One representing the Father in the earth, Jesus manifested both grace, that is, God's love and favor for all mankind, offering salvation to the whole world and also the fullness of truth - The Truth. Without both components of grace and truth operating in our lives we are liable to become unbalanced, unstable and less effective in the Kingdom of God.

Of course, God is ultimately interested in our success in all aspects of life, especially our spiritual life. It is truly by grace that we are saved, and by grace that we live. It is in truth that we walk to please the Lord in all that we do.

To close this brief study on Grace and Truth, I want to focus our attention on several significant scriptures. They speak about this great grace and marvelous truth that Jesus is and gives to us by His Spirit.

More on Grace

Grace makes it possible for us to be obedient as we operate in faith. Faith is required if we wish to please the Lord, although we are already pleasing to Him as His children. Yet faith is still a requirement, although we do not have to please the Lord for Him to love us. God's love for his children is unconditional. (See more on this in Romans 1:5, 5:2)

Hebrews 4:16 states:

> "Let us therefore draw near with confidence to the throne of grace, that we may receive mercy and may find grace to help in time of need."

There is a wonderful place that we as believers can go to when we have a need - the throne of Grace. This throne is easily reached in prayer, when we pray with the simple trust of a child.

It is the place where the Lord lives, ostensibly in our hearts.

As we come to the Lord in prayer, in the name or authority of our risen King Jesus, we can do so without fear and with great confidence. Not as the Old Testament saints did to the Mountain with Moses, but with assurance that we will be welcomed with open arms by our loving heavenly Father. We can be assured that we will receive mercy, which is new every morning. We will find help for whatever problem we may have, and find God's wonderful favor. His grace is always available for those who believe.

Grace is such a wonderful thing and has been so freely given by our Lord. Grace must be accepted in order to receive it, one would think that all would want grace in

More on Grace

order to grow and mature. This is not always the case. In James 4:6-8a we read:

"But He gives a greater grace."

Therefore it says, "God is opposed to the proud, but gives grace to the humble (taken from Ps 138:6 and Prov. 3:34). Submit therefore to God, Resist the devil and he will flee from you. Draw near to God, and He will draw near to you."

There is a greater grace to be gained through our reciprocal relationship with the Lord. As we turn our face towards Jesus, even as Jesus had his face continually faced towards the Father (John 1:1), we are changed from glory to glory. As we submit to Him, he exalts and empowers us. As we resist the devil from the place of humble submission, He defeats the enemy of our souls again and again.

Remember, I am not saying this affects God's love for us, but frankly, as hard as it is to swallow sometimes, God does pour out His favor more on some than others. Ultimately, the favor poured out by the Lord is for His glory and our good, ultimately for His greater purposes which are often unknown to us.

One thing is for certain, God is always fair. If we do our part to seek Him and humble ourselves before Him, He will lift us up in due season. We can trust Him.

This leads to my final point. Receiving grace is not a once in a lifetime event. It does not come to us on the occasion of our salvation alone, but is provided for us when we need it, at all times. By grace we are saved, stay saved, will be saved, grow, change, mature and find what pleases the Lord (Eph. 5:10).

"But grow in the grace and knowledge of
our Lord and Savior Jesus Christ. To Him be

the glory, both now and to the day of eternity. Amen."

My prayer every day is "Lord, thank you for grace given, and grace received, and thank you for helping me grow in your grace." We grow as we live to the best of our abilities, as Jesus. We are filled with grace and truth, and have grace for grace.

What is Truth?

Truth is important... it is vitally important. In Prov. 23:23 we read:

> "Buy Truth, and do not sell it, get wisdom and instruction and understanding."

Pilot questioned Jesus at his trial with the statement, "What is truth?" That was a good question. One thing is for certain, the Word of God, when it is properly understood, is the truth by which we are to live. Thus, Solomon urges us to pay the cost for it. The cost is diligence in study, and faithfulness in application, leading to wisdom in life - the goal for every believer.

I am truly amazed when given the privilege to teach and observe international students in regards to their diligence in study. They often lack the resources Westerners take for granted, yet they do not allow that fact to hinder their eagerness to learn. They study as though their lives depended on it and of course they do, as do ours.

In our Western culture we may enjoy the luxury of having numerous bibles, study guides, commentaries, etc., while in many parts of the world just having a bible in one's own language is the key to life. We must learn to appreciate the gifts of grace God has given to us. We

What is Truth?

must be willing to pay the price to know the word and to grow in knowledge. This leads to our understanding and ultimately to the application of knowledge and understanding, which is wisdom.

Paul reiterates this principle when he categorically states that the Gospel is truth (Gal. 2:5). The good news, embodied in the death, burial, and resurrection of Jesus Christ is the most important and vital truth of all. We can know the truth that sets us free when we receive it by the simple act of the confession of our faith. This is truth, for truth is more than facts and figures, it is in a relationship with Jesus.

Of course, the church has a great responsibility to spread the good news. The church is responsible for disseminating and demonstrating the truth, for as Paul stated, the church is the pillar and support of the truth. It must never compromise the core biblical principles on which it was established.

Remember, Jesus is building His church, expressed in the capacity of the local congregation. The church is everywhere that His people are, for His glory. Holding to a standard of righteousness in our rapidly changing culture is difficult at times, but it is the prime responsibility of the church of Jesus Christ. The church is responsible for providing the instruction in righteousness. The church is to serve by example. Of course, we can only do this by the grace or favor of God which has been amply provided to each believer.

Even when we sin, for if we say we do not sin the truth is not in us, (see 1 John 1:8) we lie; it affects our relationship with the Lord (not His love or acceptance of us). It also affects our ability to function in the Kingdom of God. So the church, with love and grace, must bring correction when it is warranted; especially if a believer does not see the errors of his or her ways. Perhaps in

Grace and Truth: We Can't Live Without Them

so doing, he will repent from obvious and grievous sin. True repentance, which is a change of thinking leading to a change in life style or pattern of behavior, is the manifestation of grace and truth for the Christian.

Finally, we must learn to handle the word with diligence (1 Tim 2:15) for the word of God, is not just words, it is God's word. Remember, "All scripture is inspired by God, and profitable for teaching, for reproof, for correction, for training in righteousness, that the man of God may be adequate, equipped for every good work."

We are the people of God, His body here on the earth. We are to let his light shine from the midst of our lives, bringing the Truth to every place and in every situation. We are the salt of the earth, a city set on a hill. We are a lighthouse to the lost, that they may be found in the loving arms of Jesus to be saved by His grace. We are the ones who lead the lost to repentance and heal the sick. This we do for the glory of God. In doing so, we help to fulfill the prophetic declaration, that the whole earth will be full of his glory.

Chapter 10

Conclusion

Grace and Truth: The Twin Towers of the Father's Heart...

Benjamin lied. He lied as habit; often lying when he didn't need to. In many ways, this was understandable, considering his early life of abandonment by parents and rejection by peers. He had bounced around from foster home to foster home, leaving him feeling less than loved and wanted.

In his late teens, Benjamin had a true encounter with Christ. He was, in his own words, "radically saved." Soon after he joined a church and enjoyed initial forgiveness but still had trouble grasping the full concept of grace - let alone truth.

As he grew in the Lord, Ben settled into the church, and, as is common for most believers, the issues of life, rooted in false beliefs, born from his early abuse and neglect, emerged. His propensity to lie when convenient and inconvenient resurfaced. He knew truth and The Truth, but struggled to walk in it, frequently suffering the consequences of the choices he made. But in time

Conclusion

truth won, as an atmosphere of grace in his church allowed the former liar to enjoy the freedom of becoming a truth seeker and liver, with the help of loving friends who confronted him with truth in grace.

It is this atmosphere of grace, where truth seeking and living out the truth is needed today. Believers need time to work through life's problems, and the church is the perfect place, designed by God, to work out our salvation with fear and trembling and grace and truth.

A Final Look

Terrorists destroyed many lives on September 11 of 2001. As the twin towers in New York tumbled down, the terrorists were guilty of taking the lives of many innocent victims. They also robbed us of important symbols of American prosperity, power, and influence. This was indeed a crushing blow to the people of this great nation, and it left many feeling vulnerable and afraid.

Yet the terrorists were unsuccessful in destroying this nation's identity. The towers that represented success, power, and prosperity may be gone, but this nation's identity remains intact. It is still based upon a fundamental truth that continues today, for we are still "One Nation under God."

Ultimately, as much as we love this nation, our primary allegiance must still remain to our creator who is Jesus Christ. We have no king but King Jesus, and all of our national allegiance must be subordinate to the Kingdom of God.

There is no terrorist attack big enough to destroy our identity in Him. Our salvation and our destiny, both as individuals and as a body, remain, regardless of what tomorrow holds. Even if this great country ceased to exist, our identity would still remain as believers in Him.

As we pause each year to pay tribute to the lives that were lost in this horrendous attack, let us not be so quick to forget the towers that remain. They are the twin towers of our Father's heart, that is, grace and truth.

Jesus, who is full of grace and truth, revealed to us the very nature and character of God our Father. He did this by the words that He spoke and the deeds that He did. These two characteristics, grace and truth, are to be seen in the church, in our homes, in our work places and in our personal lives.

Think about it. Grace, the unmerited, but extremely costly grace of God is exactly what the world is searching for, although unwittingly at times. They do not need our judgment or our criticism, but our genuine love and acceptance. After all, they were created in the image of God. They also need the truth, the truth that salvation is found in Jesus Christ.

There is a way that seems right to man, but it leads to death.

God does offer a better way - even life itself.

My hope and prayer is this:

Once grace is manifested and the truth is lived, it will once again be the testimony of the body; it will be a testimony of the church. It is a testimony that truly represents all of who Jesus Christ is.

May God's grace and truth be yours forever more. Amen.

Epilogue

Our study of the "Twin Towers" within the pages of this book has come to its inevitable close. Nevertheless the

Conclusion

pursuit of identity, both God's and our own must go on. As we meditate upon the truth presented within the previous pages, my hope is that the reader will stop and ask themselves, how does this truth apply to me? What does it mean to my personal journey, and how do I apply these truths to my life?

As I think back to my own upbringing, I remember the rules my parents set in place to keep me on the straight and narrow path (at least as they saw the path, with the limited light they walked in). As a youngster, there were boundaries of where and when I could come and go. There were rules that applied in regards to what I could and could not do when I was no longer in the range of their eye sight. As I proved myself to be trustworthy, they would expand the limitations to include more and more freedom.

The rules were not so much to contain me, but rather to guide me along the way until my own judgment had developed so that conscience could be my guide. Once I had become more mature, I was allowed to make decisions and choices on my own, as I had proven myself faithful over the little. I had the opportunity to learn how to make wise choices based upon the knowledge of the boundaries they had set for me in my formative years.

When we train a child in the way that he/she is to go, when they are old they will not depart from it. Parents who fail to hold their children accountable to clearly established and understood rules, show a lack of concern for them or an inadequate understanding of their important role in guiding a child in healthy patterns. Too much freedom too early, can lead to a life that lacks self-discipline. Each of us must learn self-discipline to live a successful and healthful life.

Just as we care enough about our own children to establish and enforce the rules, rules that will guide and

Epilogue

protect them, so does our Heavenly Father. His law, the law of love, was not meant to burden us, but to provide the guidance necessary for us to live life to the fullest. He established the laws of the Old Testament, and natural laws are designed to protect us from harm. Thus, the law of love, to do unto others as you would have them do unto you, etc., is meant to order our steps and light our path. He does this because as our Father, He truly cares. He cares where we end up and how we get there. He has an expected end for each one of us. and He wants to make certain we fulfill the destiny He has for us as His children.

Even though we do not always make the right choices or choose the right path, He picks us up, dusts us off, and sets us back upon the right path. He prefers the role of loving Father, not strict disciplinarian. He loves us with an everlasting love. God is love; when we listen to Him and even when we don't.

If you doubt this, look again at the story of the Prodigal son. The father waited with open arms to receive him back into his home; he even threw a party for him. He did not care where he had been or what he had done, he just cared that he was back in his father's loving arms. That is the way God is with us. He loves us no matter what.

That is why He gave us the Truth to guide us along the way. The Old Covenant framework of truth is the law, including the Ten Commandments. Paul the apostle stated in Romans 7:14 that the law is good, but the law could never save, but in fact it revealed our inability to keep the law; thus grace was needed. Through grace, the law which is still in force, the law of love in Jesus Christ, can be lived out, but only by His grace. Thus, we must remember that our Father has given us the law of love in Christ Jesus, that by Truth and Grace we might know

Conclusion

Him. By knowing Him we might also come to discover the truth of who we are in Him. Romans 2:4;

"Do you think lightly of the riches of His kindness and forbearance and patience, not knowing that the kindness (similar word to grace) of God leads you to repentance?"

The grace of God, leads us to desire the Truth which is Jesus the living Word.

Living in Grace and Truth, twin towers of the Father's heart, leads and gently guides us in the Way or the path that leads to life. This grace has been imparted to us by the faith of the Son of God, so that we can become who we already are in Christ. He loves us enough to establish, in keeping with the law of love, healthy boundaries; so that we might walk the way, while resting in the knowledge that He will always walk with us, even to the end. That is what grace and truth means to me. What does grace and truth mean to you?

I think of all the mistakes I have made in life, sometimes huge ones! There were times when I rebelliously chose the wrong path, yet He is always so faithful, waiting patiently for my return (repentance). He did not leave me, though I left Him for a season. But when I realized how lost I was (yet never out of His sight or care) and returned once again, He awaited with open arms. His kindness or grace is what draws me - not fear of punishment, but grace. This grace is certainly risky for God, for what if we just decide to continue to walk in rebellion? What if we willfully do our own thing? Well, there will be consequences, that is for sure, but His love will never fail. His grace is all sufficient, and He chose to take the risk of radical grace for the sake of real relationship, not based upon rules or fear, but grace and truth.

I am grateful that he was willing to risk it all in sending Jesus, to embody the fullness of the Father, in grace and truth. His grace makes walking in the truth and pleasing my Father, my highest goal, as it was for Jesus. May you make it your aim, knowing that His grace will enable you, for "He who has begun a good work in you will perfect it until the day of Christ Jesus."

About the Author

Dr. Stan DeKoven is the founder and President of Vision International Ministries, with programs including:

- Vision International University

- Vision International Education Network, with Learning Centers in over 150 nations worldwide.

- Vision Publishing

- Walk in Wisdom Ministries

- International Association of Christian Counseling Professionals

Further, Dr. DeKoven is the author of over 35 books and guides in practical Christian living, all of which are an outgrowth of his extensive teaching ministry both nationally and internationally.

Dr. DeKoven is a graduate of San Diego State University, (B.A. Psychology), Webster University' (M.A. Counseling), Professional School of Psychological Studies (Ph.D., Counseling Psychology) Evangelical Theological Seminary (D.Min.) and is a licensed Marriage, Family and Child Counselor. As an Ordained minister and professional caregiver and educator, he is actively establishing educational programs and counseling ministry around

About the Author

the world and equipping God's leaders to equip the saints for end-time harvest.

More of Dr. DeKoven's teachings can be found at his website www.drstandekoven.com and his books are available at www.booksbyvision.com.

www.ingramcontent.com/pod-product-compliance
Lightning Source LLC
Chambersburg PA
CBHW060847050426
42453CB00008B/873